Tomorrow We Go to Bethlehem

TOMORROW WE GO TO BETHLEHEM

Five Plays for
—— the ——
Christmas Season

Edited by John McTavish

Abingdon Press

Tomorrow We Go to Bethlehem:
Five Plays for the Christmas Season

Copyright © 1986 by Abingdon Press

Upon the purchase of one copy of this work, Abingdon Press hereby grants permission to churches to reproduce the material contained in this publication for purposes of rehearsal and performance, provided the following notice appears on each copy: From *Tomorrow We Go to Bethlehem,* edited by John McTavish. Copyright © 1986 by Abingdon Press. Used by permission.

Further, the purchase of this copy conveys rights for performance of the works included under church sponsorship, provided there is no charge for admission.

Except as noted above, no part of this work may be reproduced or transmitted in any form or by any means, electronic or mechanical, including photocopying and recording, or by any information storage or retrieval system, except as may be expressly permitted by the 1976 Copyright Act or in writing from the publisher. Requests for permission should be addressed in writing to Abingdon Press, 201 Eighth Avenue, South, Nashville, TN 37202.

Scripture quotations unless otherwise noted are from the Revised Standard Version of the Bible, copyrighted 1946, 1952, © 1971, 1973, by the Division of Christian Education of the National Council of the Churches of Christ in the U.S.A., and used by permission.

ISBN 0-687-42330-9

MANUFACTURED IN THE UNITED STATES OF AMERICA

CONTENTS

Preface 6

Tomorrow We Go to Bethlehem by Patricia Wells 7
By the magic of time-warp, a group of modern tourists arrive in Bethlehem just as Mary and Joseph come along looking for a place to stay.

A Word with You by Marney Heatley and Brian Martin 11
Simon, the shepherd, misses work one night when his wife gives birth. The same night Jesus is born and Simon's fellow workers witness strange events in the fields leading to adventure and discovery.

Christmas at the Clubhouse by Mark Reed 21
When the children can't find a Christmas tree for the clubhouse, disappointment sets in. Then they discover something that reminds them even more of the true meaning of Christmas.

The Lambs' Christmas by Philip Shore 27
Bossy shepherds and an overprotective donkey shoo the lambs away from the manger. But the little creatures still manage to celebrate a good Christmas when they realize the best gifts come from within.

For Unto Us by Earl Harrison 33
Chorale readings, dramatic vignettes and traditional Christmas music weave together to form a hour-long dramatic act of worship for Christmas Eve.

About the Authors 45

PREFACE

Christmas celebrates the miracle of the Incarnation: that infinitely startling event in which the God of the galaxies becomes one with us, breathing with our lungs, blinking in the sun with our eyes, eating our food, and experiencing firsthand, personally and intimately the joys and terrors of our human life.

The plays in this volume seek to illumine the mystery and dramatize the miracle that took place when Jesus was born. Unabashedly, they employ the very human ingredients of drama—humor, suspense, pathos, conflict—setting these to divine service, as they explore the humanity of God and the glorious nativity of his Son.

The season of Christmas is ripe for drama. Magic is in the air, and people are unusually eager and expectant. As a pastor, I have always wanted to give the congregation a Christmas present—and what more appropriate present than a play that serves up in memorable fashion the ultimate present wrapped up, for us all, in the swaddling clothes of the manger child.

Over the years I have used drama many times in my ministry. Never have I had much difficulty finding talented actors and skillful directors. Even people who normally wouldn't go near the church jump at the opportunity to get involved in a play. My problem has been finding winning scripts. That's why I gladly undertook this project for Abingdon Press. I wanted to discover outstanding scripts for my own use and, in the sharing spirit of the season, for the use of others.

Here they are.

Enjoy!

TOMORROW WE GO TO BETHLEHEM

by
Patricia Wells

CHARACTERS

TOUR GUIDE, a retired clergyman
FIRST WOMAN, tourist
SECOND WOMAN, tourist
MIDDLE-AGED HUSBAND AND WIFE, tourists
FATHER, tourist
MIKE, twelve-year-old son
JOSEPH
MARY

A group of people move up the middle aisle of the church looking around curiously. They are dressed as tourists and have the usual tourist paraphernalia—cameras, sunglasses, tote bags.

TOUR GUIDE:	And now, my good people, with this historic city of Jericho we conclude another day in our tour of the Holy Land. Are there any further questions before we move back to the bus?
FIRST WOMAN:	(*In a stage whisper to her friend*) It may be the oldest inhabited city in the world, but I can't imagine why anyone would want to live here. My lungs are clogged with dust.
SECOND WOMAN:	(*Nodding in agreement*) Right now I'd trade my soul for a nice air-conditioned hotel room.
FIRST WOMAN:	I just hope there's more hot water than when we got back last night!
SECOND WOMAN:	I know. I've certainly been on better organized tours. You'd think that if that hotel knew we were coming, they'd at least have gotten in some decent diet drinks.
GUIDE:	Right, ladies and gentlemen. I know you want to get back for a nice long soak in the tub and a little nap before dinner,

so I won't keep you any longer. Tomorrow is a very special day. Tomorrow we go to Bethlehem. The buses will be at the door by eight o'clock, so get to bed early tonight. I'll see you bright and chipper at breakfast, no later than seven. Thank you.

HUSBAND: O Lord, not another bus tour. That bus is like a blast furnace!

WIFE: I just hope he gets us back in time for some shopping tomorrow afternoon. (*They watch Mike, the only child on the tour, kick a can around.*) People shouldn't bring kids on these tours. They have no appreciation of what's going on.

The group goes off to the side, or possibly sits in the front pews. A girl in a plain brown dress or robe comes in and sits on a bench one side of the chancel, opposite to where the tourists exited. After a few seconds a young man comes in and sits beside her.

JOSEPH: I'm sorry, Mary. I've tried everything I know. We'll have to go to Bethlehem tomorrow.

MARY: I can't Joseph. You'll just have to leave me here. I'm seven months pregnant. I can't travel eighty miles over rough roads. I can't risk losing this baby. It's my first baby, and it's—very special.

JOSEPH: (*Bitterly*) Do you think that means anything to the Romans? When I asked if I could register you, they just laughed. We're a joke to them. A bad, money-making joke. We're taxes. Roman justice doesn't apply to us, Mary. Life on this earth was made for the rich. That's the way it's always been and that's the way it's always going to be.

Mary bows her head and then shakes it slowly and looks up at him.

MARY: I don't think so Joseph. I mean, I know that's how it looks, and maybe that's how it's always been, but I believe our prophets. Jehovah does see our troubles and one day—soon—he'll come to defend us. One day he will put down the mighty from their seats and lift up the poor. I know that sounds *unlikely*, but I believe it. And for now—well I guess we'll just have to manage.

Joseph puts his arm around her as they walk to the side. Tourists reenter.

GUIDE: This chapel represents the official sight where the shepherds saw the angels. There's a lovely view from here over Bethlehem. And a short way down the road (*gestures in the direction that Mary and Joseph have exited*) is the kind of

	shelter that Mary and Joseph probably stayed in. Now, this is something you'll want to tell your friends back home. Mary and Joseph probably didn't stay in what we consider a stable. It's likely they stayed in one of these small animal shelters, really just a small cave or rocky overhang where they herded the animals in bad weather.
MIKE:	(*Speaking to his father at the back of the crowd*) Dad, how many more churches do we have to look at? They're so boring!
FATHER:	Don't you realize, Mike, that this is the most important town in the world?
MIKE:	Do you really think so? Is it more important than Cape Kennedy?
FATHER:	Yes, it is.
MIKE:	Dad, will we get back to the hotel in time to see the end of the space shuttle on TV?
FATHER:	(*Exasperated*) I don't know! Mike *starts to kick the can back and forth.*
FATHER:	Look, Mike. Stop kicking that can. We brought you on this trip so you'd have some appreciation of—Christianity. This is where our faith started. That's important to me. Mike *looks at him seriously, but then after a few seconds goes back to kicking the can.*
FATHER:	(*Voice slightly raised*) Just get rid of that can!
GUIDE:	(*Speaking more animatedly, but the tour group, with the exception of Mike, begins to lose interest, and starts to look around. As the guide begins to talk Mike moves in closer to the front.*) Mary was quite young, you know, probably only about fourteen, just a kid really. Well, you can imagine that cave, with the stench from the animals, the cold, the loneliness, the pain— (*Sees his audience's attention wandering*) Yes, well it is difficult—I know most of you are eager to get back to the hotel and lunch, so we won't take time to go down there. We'll stop at the Blessed Virgin Gift Shop for a few minutes on the way out and if you want to, you can pick up a postcard of the cave. Right. Let's move along.
FIRST WOMAN:	I don't know why he wants to spoil the Christmas story for us. I think it's lovely the way it is in the Bible! *They walk off, but* Mike *remains.* Mary *and* Joseph *reenter, walking slowly.* Mike *stands to one side listening as they talk.*

9

MARY:	I can't go any farther, Joseph. I really don't feel well. Anyway, we've tried all the inns in town. There's no place else to go.
	They sit down close together on the bench looking dejected. A minute or so passes.
JOSEPH:	That last place had an animal shelter out back. I'll go ask about it. It would be better than nothing.
	He goes off briefly while Mary *remains huddled on the bench.*
JOSEPH:	(*Returning*) It's all right. Let's go. You can have my tunic for an extra blanket. It's going to be cold tonight.
MARY:	I can't take it; you'll freeze!
JOSEPH:	Come on, and don't argue. It's my tunic!
	Mary *laughs, but as* Joseph *helps her to her feet, she staggers.*
MARY:	Joseph, I'm so *scared*.
	As they go slowly off, Mike *walks up into the pulpit and reads carefully and clearly Luke 2:1-19:* "In those days a decree went out from Caesar Augustus . . ." ending with, "But Mary kept all these things, pondering them in her heart."

A WORD WITH YOU

by
Marney Heatley
and
Brian Martin

CHARACTERS

MR. MATTHEWS, manager of shepherds
BEN, MARTHA, RACHEL, SIMON, shepherds
BECKY, young stable helper
BETH, Simon's wife
BABY, Simon and Beth's baby

SCENE 1

Mr. Matthews is sitting at a desk, working diligently at some papers. Nearby on a bench, Ben, Martha, and Rachel are talking among themselves. Simon enters, carrying his lunch bucket, smiling, and walking with a bounce in his step. He approaches Mr. Matthews, who is engrossed in his work.

SIMON: (*Sheepishly*) Good morning, Mr. Matthews.

MATTHEWS: (*Without looking up*) Good morning. (*Looks up and sarcastically*) Ah, Simon. Decided to pay us a visit, did you?

SIMON: Yes, well, I'm sorry about missing work yesterday.

MATTHEWS: I hope you have a good excuse. I could use a few chuckles today.

SIMON: Well, you see, sir, it's my wife. She—

MATTHEWS: Never mind. Your absence didn't make much difference anyway. Not with all the commotion that went on up on hill twelve last night.

SIMON:	Sir?
MATTHEWS:	I'm sure you'll hear all about it before long. It's all anyone seems to be able to talk about around here. (*Pauses to write something down on a piece of paper, which he then hands to Simon*) You're working hill seven this afternoon. And keep an eye out. We've had quite a few strays lately.
SIMON:	(*Taking the paper*) Thank you, sir.
	Simon *leaves Mr. Matthews at his desk and approaches the others. They are excitedly discussing something and don't notice* Simon's *approach.*
SIMON:	Hi, guys. What's all the fuss about?
	The others jump up and start talking at once.
SIMON:	Hold on a minute. One at a time.
MARTHA:	You missed the most amazing thing last night, Simon.
SIMON:	What?
RACHEL:	It was like nothing I've ever seen before in my life.
MARTHA:	It was real cold last night, bone-chilling cold. Rachel and I were watching over Matthews' favorites, when all of a sudden this rush of warm air came out of nowhere, and there was a soft glow, sort of like moonlight, only bright enough to read by.
BEN:	This light, it covered four or five hills at least. I saw it too, and I was way over on sixteen.
RACHEL:	Then there was this flash, and a weird sort of humming noise.
BEN:	By now, the sheep were going nuts, bleating and running around like crazy.
RACHEL:	I was scared to death.
BEN:	I've seen a lot of weird things in my day, but never anything like this.
MARTHA:	And then *he* appeared.
SIMON:	Who appeared?
MARTHA:	I don't know. I guess he was an angel. All I know is that he was a messenger from God.
SIMON:	(*Entranced*) What was the message?
RACHEL:	The Savior is born. Here, in our town.

BEN: Then there were millions of these angels all singing.

RACHEL: And the weird thing was, that I knew they were singing "Glory to God," although they didn't seem to be singing words. It was like I heard it with my heart and not my ears.

BEN: It was a show like no other. The kind of thing theater producers dream about. A production number with a cast of thousands, and then they were gone (*snaps his fingers*)—just like that.

MARTHA: It was dazzling.

RACHEL: I would have thought I'd dreamed it all except for this lingering sweet smell in the air. I couldn't help feeling that I'd just witnessed the most important thing in the world.

MARTHA: Just think—the Savior! In our time and our town. How God has blessed us.

SIMON: Someone who didn't know you three as well as I do might think you'd been into the sauce last night. After all, it was pretty cold.

RACHEL: (*Insulted*) This is no time to be funny, Simon. This could be the thing we've been waiting for all our lives.

SIMON: Did you go into town then? Did you see him?

MARTHA: We tried to. We asked Mr. Matthews for permission to go, but he refused.

BEN: He said he'd heard excuses before, but this one was the best ever.

RACHEL: He told us we'd all be fired if we left the sheep.

SIMON: If what you saw was as important as you seem to think, why didn't you go anyway?

MARTHA: Oh, Simon, you know how times are. If we lose our jobs our families may starve.

RACHEL: I'd think you'd be especially concerned about that, Simon. What with Beth expecting and all.

SIMON: Oh, I meant to tell you. Beth had the baby—a girl! That's why I was away yesterday.

MARTHA: Oh, Simon, that's marvelous.

BEN: Congratulations, "Dad."

RACHEL: I guess you experienced your own little miracle last night.

SIMON: A baby is a pretty special thing.

RACHEL: Yeah.

MARTHA: We're really happy for you, Simon, but what are we going to do about this other baby?

SIMON: I think we should go into town. I don't think Mr. Matthews would fire us. He comes across as a tyrant, but he's really a nice guy.

MARTHA: Maybe, but what happens if he decides to follow through on his threat?

SIMON: Let's talk to him again.

BEN: It's worth a try. Let's go.

They approach Mr. Matthews at his desk.

MARTHA: Excuse me, sir.

MATTHEWS: What is it? Why aren't you out in the fields yet?

MARTHA: We've been talking about what happened last night. We feel that it's important that we go into town and check it out.

MATTHEWS: Listen, we've got a business to run here. I can't afford to have half a shift running off, chasing the results of the previous night's overindulgence.

SIMON: If I may, sir, I've only heard about this secondhand, but there's something about it that I can't shake loose.

RACHEL: You know us, Mr. Matthews. We wouldn't ask to go if it wasn't important.

MARTHA: We won't be long.

MATTHEWS: Who's going to tend the sheep?

BEN: John in the far field owes me a favor. I'm sure he'll keep a watch on our flocks.

MARTHA: We'd like your permission, but we're going even if you don't give it.

MATTHEWS: (*Resignedly*) Very well, but please hurry back.

MARTHA: Thank you, sir.

They all turn to go.

RACHEL: (*Turning back*) Why don't you come with us?

MATTHEWS: (*Considering and then rejecting the idea*) There's too much to do here. I really can't.

RACHEL:	Oh, come on. The place will survive without you for a few hours.
MATTHEWS:	(*Softening*) Well— (*looking at the papers on his desk*) no, I've got all these census forms to finish up. Got to keep the government happy, you know. You four go—with my good wishes.
RACHEL:	Thank you, sir.
	Shepherds *exit*.

SCENE 2

Shepherds *approach the stable, indicated by a bale or two of straw.*

BEN:	(*Pointing up*) Look, there's the star we're supposed to follow.
SIMON:	It's coming to rest over the Ritz Hotel.
MARTHA:	The Ritz, of course! We should have guessed that ourselves.
RACHEL:	Do they have mangers at the Ritz?
SIMON:	Mangers?
RACHEL:	I thought the angels said something about "lying in a manger."
MARTHA:	With all the ruckus, it was hard to tell what they were saying. They probably said—um—"lying with an angel."
BEN:	Look, the star is moving again.
	They all look up.
MARTHA:	Why is it moving? This is the best hotel in town.
SIMON:	I don't know. It's disappeared behind that turret.
BEN:	Let's go.
RACHEL:	Wait.
BEN:	What now?
RACHEL:	I'm scared. Think of the show those angels put on. That was just the introduction. Will common shepherds like us be able to look on the face of the Savior, or will it be just too much for us?
MARTHA:	That's a chance we have to take, Rachel. If God has chosen to bless us in this way, how can we refuse him?

SIMON:	What better chance have we to worship God than this?
BEN:	Let's get going before the star gets too far ahead of us.
MARTHA:	Stay or come with us, Rachel. It's your choice, but don't come whining to me if you miss the opportunity of a lifetime.
RACHEL:	I'll come.

Ben and Simon have moved a little closer to the stable. Rachel and Martha catch up to them.

SIMON:	There's the star.
RACHEL:	How come it stopped over that barn?
BEN:	Give it a minute. It'll move again.
SIMON:	I don't think so.
MARTHA:	This is ridiculous.
RACHEL:	You think we misheard about the star, too?
BEN:	We must have. Let's go back and check the hotel.
SIMON:	I'm going to see what's in the barn.
MARTHA:	Come on, Simon. It'll be a waste of time.
BEN:	I don't want to hobnob with sheep any more than I have to.

At this point, Becky comes running in, with her arms laden with swaddling clothes. She brushes past the shepherds and calls into the stable.

BECKY:	I brought the swaddling clothes, and the kitchen boy at the hotel promised to lend me his blanket.
RACHEL:	Swaddling clothes? The angels said something about swaddling clothes.
BECKY:	I'll be right back.

She leaves, brushing by the shepherds once more.

BEN:	I don't like this.
SIMON:	What do you think it means?
MARTHA:	I don't know. (*Grasping at straws, figuratively, that is*) Maybe it was all a practical joke.
RACHEL:	But all those lights and the music. How do you explain that?
BEN:	(*Tentatively*) They do it with mirrors.
SIMON:	Do you really believe that?

BEN:	(*Confused*) I don't know what I believe.
MARTHA:	Oh, Simon, I know it wasn't a joke. It was real and it was important, but now everything seems so confusing. I don't know what to think anymore.
SIMON:	What if you heard right about the manger and the swaddling clothes? What if the Son of God is really in that stable?
MARTHA:	We're poor people, Simon. We have to earn our living working with animals. We don't have any choice. Do you think that Almighty God, who can do whatever he wants, is going to choose to come into the world in a cold, smelly stable?
BEN:	Of course not. I mean, he wouldn't let his people down like that. We asked for a king.
SIMON:	Maybe we got a king. Let's look closer.
MARTHA:	Come on, guys, we're obviously in the wrong place. Let's go back and ask at the hotel.
	Martha *and* Ben *turn to go.* Becky *returns with a large blanket rumpled into a ball.*
BECKY:	Have you come to worship the baby too?
RACHEL:	We're looking for the King of the Jews.
BEN:	(*To Martha*) If he's not at the Ritz, we could check out the Park Plaza.
MARTHA:	Are you coming, Simon, Rachel?
SIMON:	I'll be along in a minute.
	Martha *and* Ben *start to go.* Rachel *looks hesitatingly at Simon and then at the other two.*
RACHEL:	(*To Martha and Ben*) Wait for me!
	Rachel *leaves with* Martha *and* Ben. Simon *stands in front of the stable with* Becky. *During the previous exchange,* Becky *has been fussing with the blanket, but it is too big for her to handle.*
BECKY:	(*To Simon*) Do you think you could help me with this? It's a bit too big for me.
SIMON:	Sure.
	He moves forward and helps her fold it.
BECKY:	Thanks.
SIMON:	Do you believe that this baby is the Son of God?

BECKY:	Uh huh.
SIMON:	How do you know?
BECKY:	I just know.
SIMON:	Nobody told you?
BECKY:	No, I guess not. *They finish folding the blanket.*
SIMON:	There. All done.
BECKY:	You could help me carry the water bucket if you wanted to. It's kinda heavy when it is full.
SIMON:	How come you're doing all this? Do you know these people?
BECKY:	Sure. They're Mary and Joseph and the baby Jesus. I met them this morning.
SIMON:	(*Picking up the bucket and carrying it a short distance*) Are you always this helpful to people you hardly know?
BECKY:	I have to do something. I'm poor, so I don't have anything else to give the baby as a present.
SIMON:	I don't have anything to give either.
BECKY:	That's okay. You helped. (*Putting the swaddling clothes in the bucket*) There. Those should soak for a while. Well, I'd better get going. If I'm away too long, my mom gets worried. Bye.
SIMON:	Bye. (*He looks into the stable thoughtfully, then gradually turns and walks away.*)

SCENE 3

Beth *is seated in a rocking chair, with her baby cradled in her arms. She is looking anxious. She gets up, goes to the window and looks out, and then sits down again. Finally,* Simon *comes in.*

BETH:	Simon! Where have you been? I've been worried sick. Simon *kisses Beth and the baby.*
SIMON:	How's the little one?
BETH:	Fine, but what about you? Ruth next door said she saw you downtown. Why weren't you at work?
SIMON:	Did you hear about the commotion in the fields last night?

BETH:	It's all over town. They say there were angels announcing the birth of the Savior.
SIMON:	That's why I was in town. I went to see him. A baby called Jesus.
BETH:	What did he look like? I imagine him looking like those little cherubs painted on the walls in the town hall.
SIMON:	Actually, he looks a lot like our baby—like any baby.
BETH:	Did he have a halo?
SIMON:	No. And he was born in a stable.
BETH:	(*Taking it in*) That wasn't what I was expecting.
SIMON:	That wasn't what any of us were expecting. Martha, Ben, and Rachel all left. They thought they were in the wrong place.
BETH:	Why did you stay?
SIMON:	I don't know—curiosity maybe. But I met a little girl there. She was helping out, fetching and carrying, worshiping in her own way. Seeing her faith made me realize how little I had.
BETH:	I guess children have a lot to teach us. They don't let things get in the way of their love.
SIMON:	It was hard to understand what I saw in that stable. Joseph and Mary— Who's ever heard of them? Poor nobodies holed up in a cold, dirty barn. Then they give birth to this child, and put him in the straw where the cows come to eat. It looked like a scene of lowly human squalor. We see it every day of our lives. It took a child's faith to make me realize that it was more than that—much more. That baby is the Son of God. (*Pausing to look at Beth and particularly the baby*) But why? Why did God choose this way to come into the world? It doesn't make sense to me.
	A moment of silence. Beth *studies the baby in her arms, and then looks up at Simon.*
BETH:	You know, maybe it does make sense.
	Simon *looks up at her. She gets up and hands him the baby. He rocks it gently looking warmly at it.*
BETH:	How could God understand us if he were to just sit up in heaven on his throne, like some people say he does?
SIMON:	(*Catching on*) But if God came to earth as a baby and grew up with us, he would know what it was like.

BETH:	Exactly.
SIMON:	But why did God come to earth as a poor child? He could reach more people as a great king, couldn't he?
BETH:	Maybe. But who touches your life more, a king or a friend?
SIMON:	I suppose we're used to tuning out the voices of authority by now, but we can't ignore one of our own.
BETH:	They say he was born last night. Just think— he has the same birthday as our little one.
SIMON:	(*Looking at the baby*) Maybe they'll grow up together. Wouldn't that be exciting?
BETH:	(*Taking the baby back and speaking to it*) I pray that you get a chance to meet this Jesus, play with him—learn a little of what he knows.
SIMON:	God knows we need some guidance. Life under Herod isn't easy for anyone, man or child.
BETH:	Well, we can be sure of some help now. God's put in a good word for us.

CHRISTMAS AT THE CLUBHOUSE

by
Mark Reed

CHARACTERS

Six children (or more), ages 8-12

Setting

Interior of a clubhouse. A cardboard backdrop colored like knotty panels of wood could bear graffiti and various old kid posters. A sign across the top, in a child's handwriting, reads: "The Super Duper Double Scoopers." Inverted five-gallon buckets, a wooden crate, an old tire, and a broken chair make perfect seats. A few toys lay scattered.

Three children, wearing coats and shivering a little, enter.

FIRST: All we need are a few bricks. We can do it.

SECOND: No way!

FIRST: Right here. We can build it right here and put a hole in the roof up there.

THIRD: Whoever heard of a fireplace in a clubhouse?

FIRST: We'll have the first one.

SECOND: No way!

THIRD: Yeh, and the first one to burn down, too.

SECOND: No way!

FIRST: So how we gonna make it warm in here?

THIRD: We don't need to. We'll just wear our coats.

SECOND: And three pair of pants and five shirts and extra socks and—

FIRST: No way! I'll freeze. Besides, long underwear makes me itch.

SECOND: At least your mom doesn't make you wear plastic bags over your socks.

THIRD: Let's talk about how we can decorate this clubhouse for Christmas.

SECOND: I found some old stuff at home we never use anymore. Some candles that have my sister's teeth marks in them and those things you shake around and make snow inside.

FIRST: We got some of those. But I think Bobby drank the water out of them. They don't work anymore.

THIRD: I think we need a tree.

FIRST/SECOND: Yeh!

SECOND: But where we gonna get one?

Two more children enter.

FOURTH: Get one what?

FIRST/SECOND/THIRD: Hi! ——— (*to Fourth*) Hi! ——— (*to Fifth*)

SECOND: A tree for our clubhouse.

FIRST: Hey, don't you guys think we could put a fireplace in here? We could get some bricks and make a hole in the roof over here—

FOURTH/FIFTH: (*Look at each other, then to him like he's crazy*) No way!

FIRST: What do you think about the tree?

FOURTH: Trees cost money.

FIRST: Maybe we could put our money together.

SECOND: No way! I got a dollar and twelve cents. And I have to buy a present for mom and dad, one for Tom, one for Bruno, and—

FIFTH: Bruno? Dogs don't get presents for Christmas.

SECOND: Bruno does, every Christmas.

FOURTH: We'd never have enough money anyway. Trees are offensive.

FIRST: You mean expensive.

FOURTH: Yeh, that too.

FIFTH: Hey, I got an idea. Let's go cut one down.

THIRD: Where? The only Christmas trees around here are in the park and they're fifteen billion times the size of this clubhouse.

FIRST:	Boy, what would Christmas be like without a tree?
	He sits down and props his chin with one hand, elbow resting on his knee. Everyone follows, copying his position. All frowning. A moment of silent thought.
FIRST:	No tree. (*sigh*)
THIRD:	No decorations on it. (*sigh*)
FOURTH:	No presents under it. (*sigh*)
FIFTH:	(*Slowly*) No lights that go on and off and on and off and on and—
SECOND:	No way! (*rising*) We gotta do something.
	All break the thinking position, sitting up straight.
FOURTH:	We can't use a tree. Maybe we could use something else.
	All return to the thinking position—propping chin with one hand, elbow on knee. Pause as they think again.
SECOND:	(*Sits up suddenly, loudly*) How about a giant present?
THIRD:	It would take too much wrapping paper. My mom's still mad about last year when we used that whole role of Santa paper to wrap up Bruno.
FIRST:	And what would we put inside it?
FIFTH:	We gotta think of something else.
	Pause.
FOURTH:	How about something that will help us remember the true meaning of Christmas.
SECOND:	A cross.
THIRD:	That's Easter.
FIFTH:	But that's why Jesus was born—to die on the cross.
FIRST:	Hey, that gives me a great idea.
OTHERS:	What?
FIRST:	Come on, I'll show you.
	All follow him out.
	Later six or more children enter carrying manger with a small, rough wooden cross extending above it, straw, and decorations. Sixth is a smaller girl carrying a doll.
FIRST:	I'm glad we found this manger. I wasn't sure it was still in our garage.

FOURTH:	It was nice of your dad to give it to us.
THIRD:	It was nice to be able to find it. Boy, I thought our garage was messy, but yours— We're lucky to come out alive.
SECOND:	Come on, let's decorate it.
	They decorate the manger and cross with tinsel, lights, and a few ornaments putting straw inside and around it.
FIFTH:	Now all we need is the baby Jesus.
	Everyone looks at Sixth who holds the doll tightly.
FIRST:	Come on, ——— (*to Sixth*) you said we could use it. Only for a couple of days.
	Sixth *looks at them, then down at her doll. Finally she surrenders and places the doll in the manger.*
SIXTH:	You'll make a good Jesus. Don't worry. I'll be right here. (*Stands beside the manger with one hand near the doll.*)
FOURTH:	That looks pretty good. Now all we need are presents to put underneath the manger.
FIRST:	Presents?
THIRD:	Like presents for Jesus.
FIFTH:	This is a lot better than a tree. It helps us remember what Christmas is all about.
FOURTH:	The cross was a good idea. The manger and the cross—that tells the whole story.
	Pause.
FIRST:	Hey, why don't we put on a play about Jesus' birth? I know where we can get some costumes.
SIXTH:	I want to be Mary! It's my doll.
FOURTH:	I'm Joseph.
FIFTH:	I guess the rest of us are shepherds. I'm always a shepherd.
THIRD:	What about the three kings? That's what I want to be.
FIRST:	I'll be one!
FOURTH:	Me too!
THIRD:	You're Joseph. You can't be both.
FIFTH:	What about shepherds? We need some more shepherds.
SECOND:	Not me. Nooo waaay!

FIRST: I bet I could get my cousins.

SECOND: What about me? Can I be an angel?

All ignore Second.

FOURTH: *(To First)* Not the ones who ruined our play about Noah.

FIRST: It wasn't their fault the pigs got loose.

THIRD: My mom nearly had a heart attack when they knocked her chair over.

SECOND: *(Standing straight and tall, hands out with palms up; a soft, kind voice with serious expression)* "Behold, I bring you good tidings of great joy."

FOURTH: *(Ignoring Second)* We'll find someone else to help.

SECOND: An angel fits my personality. Can I be an angel? *(Loudly)* Listen everybody. *(Everyone suddenly turns to him)* Can I be an angel?

OTHERS: *(In rehearsed unison)* No way!

All exit leaving Second behind who finally runs out after them.

THE LAMBS' CHRISTMAS

by
Philip Shore

CHARACTERS

FIRST SHEPHERD
SECOND SHEPHERD
MARTHA, THEOPHILUS, REBECCA, BILDAD, sheep
DONKEY
FIRST ANGEL
OTHER ANGELS, as many as can be mustered

A curtain is placed across the front of the chancel/stage. Behind the curtain is the manger with doll on straw; ten feet or so away from the manger is the stall represented by a cardboard box (refrigerator or washing machine size).

At open: the curtains are closed. Behind the curtains the angels wait. The First Angel will appear over the top of the curtain by standing on ladder. (If this is not possible, the ladder is pulled out from behind the curtain and the angel mounts it.)

Angels (young and very young children) wear white choir robes and garlands of gold or silver tinsel around heads. If robes are not available, simply trim dress with the tinsel.

Out front, two shepherds herd in the sheep, four of them. The sheep wear blue jeans and solid color tops and tennis shoes. They have sheep tails and sheep ears. One sheep has a black tail. Sheep need not move on all fours: they should leap and gambol where appropriate, holding their hands in front as people do when imitating rabbits.

The sheep willingly go where they are herded and stay in a clump no matter what. They bleat and one runs away into the audience. One of the shepherds brings it back.

FIRST SHEPHERD: This looks like a good place.

SECOND SHEPHERD: Yep.

FIRST SHEPHERD:	Let's bed 'em down.
SECOND SHEPHERD:	(*Nods*) Sheep!

All sheep *turn to* shepherd.

SECOND SHEPHERD:	Sleep!

All sheep *sleep with much snoring and whistling. The* shepherds *sit down and nod off to sleep. The* first angel *pops her head over the curtain rail. She clears her throat. The* shepherds *sleep. She rings a bell. The* shepherds *start awake. When they see the* angel, *they are afraid.*

FIRST ANGEL:	"Be not afraid; for, behold, I bring you good news of a great joy which will come to *all* the people; for, to you is born this day in the city of David a Savior who is Christ the Lord. And this will be a sign to you: you will find a babe wrapped in swaddling cloths and lying in a manger."

The other angels *come from behind the curtain and surround the astonished shepherds.*

ALL ANGELS:	Glory to God in the highest heaven and on earth peace, goodwill toward men.

The angels *disperse into audience.*

FIRST ANGEL:	(*After the rest of the angels are at their seats*) Glory to God in the highest heaven and on earth, peace goodwill toward men.
FIRST SHEPHERD:	Let's go straight to Bethlehem and see this thing which the Lord has made known to us.

They go offstage. The sheep *who woke up during the* angels *speaking notice they have been abandoned.*

MARTHA:	Wait.
THEOPHILUS:	Don't leave us.
REBECCA:	We're coming too.
BILDAD:	Wait.

The sheep *go offstage after the* shepherds. *The curtain opens and there is a* donkey *eating hay in the stall, upstage left. The donkey is represented by jean and sweatshirt-clad human being with ears fastened on. Downstage right is a manger with a doll representing the baby Jesus. The* donkey *looks tired. The* sheep *enter.*

MARTHA:	(*Loudly*) Have you seen our shepherds?

DONKEY:	Ssssh! The baby is asleep.
THEOPHILUS:	What baby?
REBECCA:	Where's its mama?
BILDAD:	What a nice baby.
DONKEY:	Get away from that manger. Come over here. What do you want?
MARTHA:	We want our shepherds. We're lost without them.
DONKEY:	I think I know who you mean. They were here but are gone now. This is such a busy place lately.
THEOPHILUS:	Looks pretty quiet now.
DONKEY:	First the babe was born. Then the Wise Men came. Then your shepherds.
REBECCA:	That's a lot of visitors.
DONKEY:	And all because of the baby.
BILDAD:	It's a cute baby.
DONKEY:	He will be the Lord of the world.
BILDAD:	That little thing?
DONKEY:	It has been foretold a long time. This is Jesus the Anointed One.
THEOPHILUS:	(*Bleats in awe*) Bah ah aha aha.
DONKEY:	The Wise Men brought expensive presents. Every one who drops in brings presents. I don't know what we're going to do with them.
MARTHA:	I want to give something.
REBECCA:	Me too.
BILDAD:	Me too.
THEOPHILUS:	What can *we* give?
DONKEY:	One little boy came in and played his drum for baby Jesus.
THEOPHILUS:	Did it make him cry?
DONKEY:	The baby liked it. It hurt my ears.
THEOPHILUS:	What can *we* give?
DONKEY:	Make it light, please. I think we're going to Egypt in a few days and I do all the carrying.

BILDAD:	I'll warm the baby with my breath. (*Goes to the manger and then returns.*)
MARTHA:	What's wrong?
BILDAD:	He didn't need warming. The air is so bright around him.
REBECCA:	I'll give him my wool.
MARTHA:	How will you give him your wool. Somebody has to cut it off and prepare it. That's not something you can give.
THEOPHILUS:	What else?
REBECCA:	What else?
BILDAD:	What else?

The shepherds enter front stage right.

FIRST SHEPHERD:	(*As they come in*) Glory be to God on high.
SECOND SHEPHERD:	Praised be the name of the Lord.
FIRST SHEPHERD:	Our sheep! I had forgotten all about them.
SECOND SHEPHERD:	What are they doing here?
FIRST SHEPHERD:	We've got to get back to our job.
SECOND SHEPHERD:	Move along, little animals. Let's go.
MARTHA:	I'm not ready.
THEOPHILUS:	We haven't given a present yet.
FIRST SHEPHERD:	Let's go. Come on little sheep.
REBECCA:	Not yet.
BILDAD:	Not yet.
ALL SHEEP:	Bahhahahahahah.

The shepherds move the sheep farther to left. The curtain is closed on the donkey and the manger. The hillside again. The shepherds and sheep return to stage center.

FIRST SHEPHERD:	Glory be to God! What an honor to be told of the coming of the Lord.

SECOND SHEPHERD:	What a responsibility. We have to tell others.
FIRST SHEPHERD:	Our word may be doubted.
SECOND SHEPHERD:	But we know the truth. Let's try to get some rest.
FIRST SHEPHERD:	Sheep!

All sheep *turn to the* shepherd.

FIRST SHEPHERD:	Sleep!

All sheep *go to sleep. The* shepherds *sit down and again fall asleep. The* sheep *wake up as soon as the* shepherds *are asleep.* Martha *first and then the others move a little distance away.*

BILDAD:	We didn't give any presents.
REBECCA:	There wasn't time.
THEOPHILUS:	Is there anything we can do?
MARTHA:	I have an idea, but it's sort of complicated.
REBECCA:	What is it?
MARTHA:	We don't have any *things* we can give. Right?
BILDAD:	Right.
MARTHA:	Someone's always herding us one way or another.
THEOPHILUS:	Right!
MARTHA:	And he'll be gone by the time any of us can get back to Bethlehem. We may never see him again.
THEOPHILUS:	True.
MARTHA:	But he is in our hearts and from there he'll never leave.
BILDAD:	So?
MARTHA:	So let's give presents from our hearts to his—things we know he'll like, even though he'll never know we gave them.
THEOPHILUS:	(*After a moment's thought*) I will dedicate my hooves to his service.
REBECCA:	I will dedicate my eyes to his service.
BILDAD:	My every thought will be his.

MARTHA:	I will live my life in his service.
BILDAD:	These are fine gifts.
REBECCA:	And the donkey can't complain about the weight.
THEOPHILUS:	We need to get some rest.
MARTHA:	Tomorrow let's tell all the other sheep about the King, Jesus the Anointed One.
BILDAD:	Good night.
REBECCA:	Good night.
THEOPHILUS:	Good night.
MARTHA:	Good night.

They form their little knot. One head peeps up.

REBECCA:	Glory to God in the highest!

FOR UNTO US

A Dramatic Act of Worship for Christmas Eve

by
Earl Harrison

Based on and adapted from the Revised Standard Version of the Bible. Direct quotations from the RSV appear in italics. Quotations from the RSV copyrighted 1946, 1952, © 1971, 1973, by the Division of Christian Education of the National Council of the Churches of Christ in the U.S.A., and used by permission.

CHARACTERS / READERS

MARY	JOSEPH
MALE CHORUS	FEMALE CHORUS
MALE 1	FEMALE 1

The scene is a manger; the staging can be as simple or as elaborate as desired.

The narrative parts, both solo and chorus, may be read; the lines spoken by Mary and Joseph should be memorized.

Just before the service begins, the lights sould be briefly turned out, so the male and female choruses can take their places on either side of the manger scene; they may stand or sit on stools. Once they are in place the lights should be turned on but kept as dim as possible so that they can see the words and music of the hymns.

Joseph and Mary, once they have entered the scene, should remain motionless, as though reflecting, during the reading of the narrative passages and the singing of the hymns.

The hymns and anthems included are intended as suggestions only; others may be selected according to familiarity and availability.

CALL TO WORSHIP
MALE/FEMALE CHORUS:
> *For to us a child is born,*
> *to us a son is given;*
> *and the government will be upon his shoulder,*
> *and his name will be called*
> *"Wonderful Counselor, Mighty God,*
> *Everlasting Father, Prince of Peace."*

HYMN: "O Come, O Come, Emmanuel"

MALE 1:	*Now the birth of Jesus Christ took place in this way.*
FEMALE 1:	*When his mother Mary had been bethrothed to Joseph, before they came together she was found to be with child . . .*
MALE 1:	*and her husband Joseph, being a just man and unwilling to put her to shame, resolved to divorce her quietly.*
FEMALE 1:	*But as he considered this, behold, an angel of the Lord appeared to him in a dream, saying,*
MALE 1:	*"Joseph, son of David, do not fear to take Mary your wife,*
FEMALE 1:	*for that which is conceived in her is of the Holy Spirit;*
MALE 1:	*she will bear a son, and you shall call his name Jesus,*
FEMALE 1:	*for he will save his people from their sins."*
MALE CHORUS:	*All this took place to fulfil what the Lord had spoken by the prophet: "Behold, a virgin shall conceive and bear a son, and his name shall be called Emmanuel" (which means, God with us).*
FEMALE CHORUS:	*When Joseph woke from sleep, he did as the angel of the Lord commanded him; he took his wife, but knew her not until she had borne a son; . . . Jesus.*
ANTHEM:	*"Gentle Joseph, Mary Mild"*
MALE 1:	*In those days a decree went out from Caesar Augustus that all the world should be enrolled.*
FEMALE 1:	*This was the first enrollment, when Quirinius was governor of Syria.* About this time, as the narrative continues, Mary and Joseph *come from offstage, preferably through the congregation and make their way toward the manger. They may be dressed in period costumes or in jeans and peasant dress. Their movements suggest hesitancy and some fear, though* Joseph *tries to feign confidence.*
MALE 1:	*And all went to be enrolled, each to his own city.*
FEMALE 1:	*And Joseph also went up from Galilee, from the city of Nazareth, to Judea, to the city of David, which is called Bethlehem, because he was of the house and lineage of David,*
MALE 1:	*to be enrolled with Mary, his betrothed, who was with child.* Joseph *and* Mary *continue toward center stage, as the choruses chant mockingly.*

FEMALE CHORUS: No room, no room.

MALE CHORUS: No room, no room.

FEMALE CHORUS: Peasants.

MALE CHORUS: Riffraff.

FEMALE CHORUS: Should have planned ahead.

MALE CHORUS: Made self-provision.

Joseph and Mary get almost to the manger area and look around in dismay.

MARY: But surely—

JOSEPH: *(With some anger)* Look, there must be a place. *(Pauses, then continues, obviously hoping for a sympathetic response)* My wife's about to give birth.

FEMALE CHORUS: *(Derisively)* Try the manger.

MALE CHORUS: Use the stable.

After some moments Mary and Joseph move to the manger area and settle themselves, clearly more troubled than ever.

JOSEPH: *(Now speaking quietly, but obviously finding it hard to hide his bitterness)* Not exactly where you'd expect the Messiah.

MARY: *(Her tone understanding but pleading)* Joseph—

JOSEPH: A fine time for a new tax program.

MARY: God will use it for good.

JOSEPH: Let's hope so.

MARY: Please don't be discouraged *(pauses before continuing)*, I need you.

JOSEPH: *(With a forced laugh)* For what? I'm nothing but on the sidelines. Not much part of things at all.

MARY: *(With quiet emphasis)* You're very much part of things. You're my support.

JOSEPH: Maybe. But I'm still not sure what's going on.

MARY:	I suspect it's all being revealed.
JOSEPH:	More of your women's words.
MARY:	So?
JOSEPH:	So I wish I were more in charge of things.
MARY:	It's hard to feel in charge of birth. It just happens—when it's time.
JOSEPH:	I know. But still I wonder. (*Pauses, then continues*) Are you sure—?
MARY:	(*As though she senses a question that she's heard before*) That I've known no man?
JOSEPH:	(*As though continuing to wrestle with traces of doubt but refusing to give in*) About the message you heard.
MARY:	(*As though trying to be understanding*) Are you not sure of the one which came to you?
JOSEPH:	Please tell me yours again.
MARY:	(*After some moments*) I remember well what was said.
MALE CHORUS:	"Hail, O favored one, the Lord is with you!"
FEMALE CHORUS:	"Do not be afraid, Mary, for you have found favor with God.
MALE CHORUS:	And behold, you will conceive . . . and bear a son, and you shall call his name Jesus.
FEMALE CHORUS:	He will be great, and will be called the Son of the Most High;
MALE CHORUS:	and the Lord God will give to him the throne of his father David,
FEMALE CHORUS:	and he will reign over the house of Jacob for ever."
MARY:	(*After some moments, as though to herself as well as to Joseph*) And I cried out—I really did: "How shall this be, since I have no husband?"
MALE CHORUS:	"The Holy Spirit will come upon you, and the power of the Most High will overshadow you;
FEMALE CHORUS:	therefore the child to be born will be called holy, the Son of God."
JOSEPH:	(*After some moments*) I do not doubt you.

MARY:	(*Somewhat anxiously*) Wasn't it the same as the message you heard?
JOSEPH:	(*After some moments*) In essence, yes.
MARY:	(*Reassured for the moment*) It seemed so wondrous at the time. I sang out, "Behold, I am the handmaid of the Lord; let it be to me according to your word."
HYMN:	"Come, Thou Long-Expected Jesus"
MALE 1:	*In the days of Herod, king of Judea, there was a priest named Zechariah, . . .*
FEMALE 1:	*and he had a wife . . . and her name was Elizabeth.*
MALE 1:	*And they were both righteous before God, walking in all the commandments and ordinances of the Lord blameless.*
FEMALE 1:	*But they had no child, because Elizabeth was barren, and both were advanced in years.*
MALE 1:	*Now while he was serving as priest. . . , it fell to him by lot to enter the temple of the Lord. . . . And there appeared to him an angel of the Lord standing on the right side of the altar of incense.*
FEMALE 1:	*And Zechariah was troubled when he saw him, and fear fell upon him.*
MALE 1:	*But the angel said to him, "Do not be afraid, Zechariah, your prayer is heard,*
FEMALE 1:	*and your wife Elizabeth will bear you a son, and you shall call his name John . . . ."*
MALE 1:	*Zechariah said to the angel, "How shall I know this? For I am an old man, and my wife is advanced in years."*
FEMALE 1:	*And the angel answered him, "I am Gabriel, who stand in the presence of God; and I was sent to speak to you, and to bring you this good news."*
MALE CHORUS:	*In those days Mary arose and went with haste into the hill country, to a city of Judah, and she entered the house of Zechariah and greeted Elizabeth.*
FEMALE CHORUS:	*And when Elizabeth heard the greeting of Mary, the babe leaped in her womb;*
MALE CHORUS:	*and Elizabeth was filled with the Holy Spirit and she exclaimed with a loud cry,*

FEMALE CHORUS:	"Blessed are you among women, and blessed is the fruit of your womb! . . .
MALE CHORUS:	And blessed is she who believed that there would be a fulfilment of what was spoken of her from the Lord."
FEMALE CHORUS:	And Mary said—
MARY:	(*Speaking the Magnificat as though in a kind of reverie, or alternatively singing the Magnificat*)

"My soul magnifies the Lord,
and my spirit rejoices in God my Savior,
for he has regarded the low estate of his handmaiden.
For behold, henceforth all generations will call me blessed;
for he who is mighty has done great things for me,
and holy is his name.
And his mercy is on those who fear him
from generation to generation.
He has shown strength with his arm,
he has scattered the proud in the imagination of their hearts,
he has put down the mighty from their thrones,
and exalted those of low degree;
he has filled the hungry with good things,
and the rich he has sent empty away.
He has helped his servant Israel,
in remembrance of his mercy,
as he spoke to our fathers,
to Abraham and to his posterity for ever."

JOSEPH:	(*After some moments*) It's a beautiful song.
MARY:	(*Quietly*) It seemed so at the time.
MALE CHORUS:	(*Mockingly*) But now—
FEMALE CHORUS:	(*In a similar tone*) But now—
ANTHEM:	"The Cherry Tree Carol"
MARY:	(*After the anthem*) Joseph?
JOSEPH:	I'm here.
MALE CHORUS:	And we are too.

FEMALE CHORUS: We who have no time.

MALE CHORUS: We who have room only for ourselves.

FEMALE CHORUS: We who cannot be bothered.

MALE CHORUS: With questions of eternity.

FEMALE CHORUS: With matters mysterious.

MARY: (*After some moments*) Are you frightened?

JOSEPH: (*Feigning indifference*) Maybe a little.

MARY: I am too. And discouraged.

JOSEPH: (*With a little more candor*) It's hard not to be.

MARY: Somehow it's not quite as I expected.

JOSEPH: Will the birth be soon?

MARY: I think not for a little while yet.

JOSEPH: Then maybe we should get some rest.

MARY: (*Sincerely*) You're a kind man, Joseph.

JOSEPH: (*As though not being reassured but wanting to reassure*) Let's try to get some sleep.

They rearrange themselves to suggest sleep.

MALE CHORUS: Each moment is of the past—

FEMALE CHORUS: And of the future—

MALE CHORUS: Of now—

FEMALE CHORUS: Of eternity—

HYMN: "The First Noel"

MALE CHORUS: *Hear then, O house of David!*

FEMALE CHORUS: *Is it too little for you to weary men,*

MALE CHORUS: *that you weary my God also?*

FEMALE CHORUS: *Therefore the Lord himself will give you a sign.*

MALE CHORUS: *Behold, a young woman shall conceive*

FEMALE CHORUS: *and bear a son,*

MALE CHORUS: *and shall call his name Immanuel.*

FEMALE CHORUS: *which means,*

MALE CHORUS: *God with us.*

FEMALE CHORUS: But the coming will not be easy.

MALE CHORUS: Nor without grief.

FEMALE 1: *He was despised and rejected by men;*

MALE 1: *a man of sorrows, and acquainted with grief;*

FEMALE CHORUS: *he was despised, and we esteemed him not.*

MALE CHORUS: *He was oppressed, and he was afflicted,*

FEMALE CHORUS: *yet he opened not his mouth;*

MALE CHORUS: *he was wounded for our transgressions,*

FEMALE CHORUS: *he was bruised for our iniquities;*

MALE CHORUS: *And they made his grave with the wicked.*

MARY: (*As though in sleep*) Stop it. I can't bear it.

JOSEPH: (*Also as though in sleep, in agony*) It doesn't make sense.

HYMN: "It Came upon a Midnight Clear"

MARY: (*Now half awake*) Joseph?

JOSEPH: (*Irritably*) What is it?

MARY: Did you hear voices?

JOSEPH: Maybe.

MARY: (*After some moments*) It must have been a dream.

JOSEPH:	(*Perplexed, still irritated*) Look, how can this be? In a stable, in a manger.
MARY:	Joseph, please—
JOSEPH:	Consider the odds.
MARY:	(*Wearily*) Go on.
JOSEPH:	We were told to expect Messiah. Right?
MARY:	(*With a sigh*) Yes.
JOSEPH:	(*As though to emphasize*) God among us.
MARY:	That was the message.
JOSEPH:	A Savior.
MARY:	I admit—
JOSEPH:	The deliverer.
MARY:	Would you stop.
JOSEPH:	(*With quiet intensity, still troubled, frustrated, perplexed*) But wouldn't such a birth be more spectacular?
MARY:	You tell me.
JOSEPH:	(*Persisting*) More political. Better planned.
MARY:	I have no answers.
JOSEPH:	Surely more dramatic.
MARY:	(*With some anger*) Look, I don't know.
HYMN:	"O Little Town of Bethlehem"
MALE CHORUS:	*Who has believed what we have heard?*
FEMALE CHORUS:	*And to whom has the arm of the Lord been revealed?*
MALE CHORUS:	*The Lord is sure,*
FEMALE CHORUS:	*making wise the simple.*
MALE CHORUS:	*We despised him;*
FEMALE CHORUS:	*we held him of no account.*
MALE CHORUS:	*In weakness*

FEMALE CHORUS:	there is strength.
MALE CHORUS:	*And with his stripes*
FEMALE CHORUS:	*we are healed.*
JOSEPH:	(*After some moments, speaking as though to himself as well as to Mary*) In essence there is no choice.
MARY:	(*Nodding*) But to trust.
MALE CHORUS:	*For as the heavens are higher than the earth,*
FEMALE CHORUS:	*so are my ways higher than your ways,* saith the Lord.
JOSEPH:	(*Quietly, to Mary*) I sense the time has come.
MARY:	(*After some moments*) Yes.
JOSEPH:	(*Hovering over her, obviously wanting to comfort*) It will be all right.
MARY:	(*As the lights become dimmer*) Oh, I hope so.
HYMN:	(*To be played through once, in the darkness*)
	"Angels from the Realms of Glory" or "While Shepherds Watched Their Flocks by Night"
	The hymn is sung after the lights go on again; Mary is seen with her arms cradled, as though holding an infant. The Male Chorus begins to speak after the hymn has been completed.
MALE CHORUS:	*There were shepherds out in the field,*
FEMALE CHORUS:	*keeping watch over their flock by night.*
MALE CHORUS:	*And an angel of the Lord appeared to them,*
FEMALE CHORUS:	*and the glory of the Lord shone around them,*
MALE CHORUS:	*and they were filled with fear.*
FEMALE CHORUS:	*And the angel said to them,*
MALE CHORUS:	*"Be not afraid; for behold, I bring you good news*

FEMALE CHORUS: *of a great joy which will come to all the people;*

MALE CHORUS: *for to you is born this day in the city of David a Savior, who is Christ the Lord.*

FEMALE CHORUS: *And this will be a sign for you: you will find a babe wrapped in swaddling cloths and lying in a manger."*

MALE CHORUS: *And suddenly there was with the angel a multitude of the heavenly host praising God and saying,*

FEMALE CHORUS: *"Glory to God in the highest,
and on earth peace among men with whom he is pleased!"*

MARY: (*To Joseph*) Well?

JOSEPH: He's a real child.

MARY: You're surprised?

JOSEPH: (*After some moments*) I guess I didn't know what to expect.

MARY: (*With quiet joy*) Well, I was expecting a baby. And he came.

JOSEPH: God with us.

MARY: That was the promise.
They embrace.

MALE/FEMALE CHORUS: *And the Word became flesh and dwelt among us, full of grace and truth; we have beheld his glory, glory as of the only Son from the Father.*

The light shines in the darkness, and the darkness has not overcome it.

ANTHEM: "Somerset Carol"

OFFERING AND DEDICATION PRAYER

THE LORD'S PRAYER

CLOSING HYMN: "Joy to the World"

BENEDICTION

ABOUT THE AUTHORS

Patricia Wells is a free-lance writer and editor of a development education publication, *The International Forum*. In reply to the question, "What was your most memorable Christmas?" she writes:

"The Christmas which comes first to mind is one, or rather a series, which were pared down to their barest bones, no glitter, not a shred of commercialism. Our family was living in the tiny Southern African Kingdom of Lesotho, where Christmas celebrations are not a traditional part of the culture. [We forget how *dismally* the Church Fathers failed when, in their wisdom, they decided to put the Christ Mass at the winter solstice and so tone down those riotous midwinter celebrations!] Christmas in Lesotho was simply a church service, like any other church service, on Christmas morning. Our tree was a few evergreen branches in a pottery jug, covered with homemade decorations. We made Christmas cookies and invited friends over after church.

"Christmas Eve we went caroling around the wards of the local hospital—*old* English carols—the Anglican chaplain who led the singing was very English. Maybe it was an imposition of our culture on the Basotho, but on Christmas Eve, unbidden, I still see the radiantly happy faces of the mothers lying with their new babies and thanking us for our songs.

"For a few years we were brought abruptly up against the question of what another baby, also in unadorned circumstances, was all about."

Marney Heatley studied creative writing at the Banff School of Fine Arts and has written a number of short stories as well as plays for Sumwat Theatre, CKMS Radio Drama and Theatre Network.

"The first year I was back in Waterloo, I had my own Christmas tree for the first time. It wasn't very big, reaching only to about my shoulder, but it was real and smelled wonderful. I had no lights or tinsel or decorations of any kind so I had a party, instructing my guests to decorate the tree. Decorations miraculously emerged from bits of paper, piles of yarn, and bowls of popcorn. On the top of the tree was a lopsided star made out of cardboard and an empty toilet paper roll. It was the most beautiful Christmas tree I'd ever seen."

Brian Martin graduated with a Bachelor of Mathematics from the University of Waterloo, Ontario, and looks forward to teaching high school mathematics.

"I fondly remember just this past Christmas, when I organized a game of Martin Trivial Pursuit. As well as recalling a lot of embarrassing anecdotes, the whole family relived many great moments together."

Mark Reed is a youth minister at the Christian Church in Ramsey, Illinois. The author of *Cave Christians and Other Skits* (Contemporary Drama Service,

1984), he has written and directed over sixty skits and plays for churches and colleges.

"Last Christmas my wife and I tramped through a foot of snow with our two-year-old looking for a Christmas tree. Usually we chose a tree from the lot at the supermarket. This time we hunted our own in the woods. We were nearly exhausted from hiking before we found the perfect tree. Chopping it down was simple. But hauling it (and my daughter) back to the car (if we could remember which way the car was). . . . We had stripped down to one layer of clothing and our sweat was producing a second foot of snow. At home the tree seemed less full than it did outdoors (almost bare to tell the truth). Still, it was *ours*. We labored hard over it. It was the best tree we ever had."

Philip Shore is the minister of a Methodist parish in Burnsville, North Carolina.

"Though I participated in the goings-on annually, I felt, for many years, estranged from Christmas. But the spirit [the Spirit?] returned when I became a parent. Giving to children, telling them the story, establishing family traditions—all these things have brought Christmas back."

Earl Harrison lives in Winnipeg, Manitoba, and is the author of numerous chancel dramas.

"I find it hard to identify *the* most memorable anything, but a significant Christmas for me was the one in 1984. It was the first year that both of our children had been away from home—about 1,300 miles away, to be exact—Lynn working, Chris going to the university. My wife, Carol, and I had not been having any special trouble with the 'empty nest syndrome' but we were certainly aware of our changed situation. And so when Lynn and Chris did come home—after some doubt that Lynn would make it because of her work—we knew that we were gathering as a family in something of a new way. For me, therefore, it ranks as a memorable Christmas, and one for which I give thanks."

John McTavish is the minister of Calvary Memorial United Church, Kitchener, Ontario.

"Along with our own three children, my wife and I had three foster children living with us one year. Christmas Eve found all eight of us gathered in the living room of our home. Marion was reading the kids a bedtime story when the front door swung open and who should walk in but a red-suited, white-bearded gentleman looking for all the world like Santa Claus. Our own three laughed in recognition; our foster children dropped their mouths in sheer amazement. Santa sat down on the Chesterfield and invited Tommy and Jessica to sit on his knee while he cradled little Crystal in his arms. Sandra, Todd, and Ian snuggled up close beside them.

"There weren't a lot of boisterous ho, ho, hos. There weren't any presents. Just Santa and the kids sitting there on our saggy Chesterfield, drinking in the love and wonder of the night.

"The memory still fetches tears to my eyes."